6. TOP, TAIL AND OVERCOAT

Text by Barbara Cooper

Illustrations by Maggie Raynor

Series consultant: Valerie Watson

Compass Equestrian

© Compass Equestrian Limited 1996
Setting by HRJ
Origination by Dot Gradations
Printed in England by Westway Offset

ISBN 1 900667 05 3

British Library Cataloguing in Publication Data.

A catalogue record for this book is available from the British Library.

A pony's overcoat – the hair on his body – helps to keep him warm and to protect his skin from injury. As it is full of grease, it is also waterproof and helps to keep him dry.

The coat changes with the weather. It is short and smooth in summer, long and thick in winter. In the spring he sheds his winter coat and thick clumps of hair fall out, which is known as 'moulting'.

Sometimes a pony's winter coat may look a different colour from that of his summer coat.

If a pony is not well, his coat will be dull, but the coat of a healthy pony will gleam.

The strong, wiry hair that grows along the ridge of a pony's neck is called his 'mane'. Most ponies have long manes which are used for flicking away flies in summer and for keeping their necks warm in winter. When a pony's mane is short and bristly it means that he has been rubbing it a lot.

Ponies with Arab blood have fine, silky manes which grow neatly on one side of their neck (usually the right-hand side).

Ponies who come from colder countries have very thick manes which sometimes flop about on both sides of their necks.

A pony's forelock (the part of the mane that falls forward between his ears) can grow long enough to cover his eyes, but it doesn't stop him from seeing.

Nearly all ponies have extra hair called 'feather' growing down the backs of their legs and over their heels. The feather grows longer and thicker in winter, and helps to protect their legs from the cold and wet. Some ponies have thick, coarse feather; others have fine, silky feather.

A pony's tail is made of the same type of strong, wiry hair as his mane. It grows from the end of his spine, and if it is allowed to grow naturally the hair fans out across his hind quarters. If the tail is not trimmed with scissors it will go on growing longer and longer. The top of the tail, called 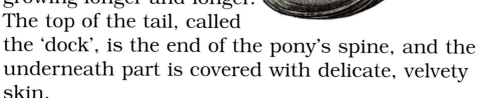 the 'dock', is the end of the pony's spine, and the underneath part is covered with delicate, velvety skin.

A pony makes use of his tail whether he is standing still or on the move. When he is jumping, it helps him to keep his balance.

When a pony is standing in a field or a yard he uses his tail to flick away flies. Often two ponies will stand head-to-tail so that they can brush the flies off each other's faces with their tails.

Sometimes a cow – or another pony – will spoil a tail by chewing the end of it so that it looks like a worn-out witch's broom.

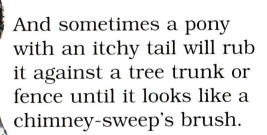

And sometimes a pony with an itchy tail will rub it against a tree trunk or fence until it looks like a chimney-sweep's brush.

By watching a pony's tail you can learn a lot about him.

Some ponies don't like being groomed, so they swish their tails about like angry cats.

Excited ponies stick their tails up high in the air like flags.

Cold, tired and frightened ponies clamp their tails down between their hind legs.

A pony who is happy with his rider will have a gently swinging tail.

A pony whose rider is making him feel uncomfortable will swish his tail briskly from side to side.

If a pony is annoyed by something (or someone) behind him he will swish his tail as a warning.

9

A pony's skin – which you don't usually see because it is covered with hair – is quite tough. It also stretches, like elastic, and he can twitch it to shake off flies which have landed on him.

Some ponies have thick skins and don't mind how you groom their coats. Others, such as chestnuts, sometimes have thin skins and can't bear being brushed too hard (which hurts them) or too gently (which tickles them).

A pony's skin is designed differently from that of other animals. When ponies are hot, they sweat all over their bodies, except for their legs. Ponies with pink skin are particularly sensitive and are likely to suffer from sunburn.

Unlike with a cat or a dog, you can feel and see the sweat on a pony – especially when there is lather (like white soap suds) caused by tack or harness rubbing on the pony's sweaty coat.

Ponies' coats, manes and tails come in many different colours and shades.

The most commonly seen colour is known as 'bay'. It may be light bay, bright bay, or bay/brown. All bay ponies have black manes and tails; their legs, from just above the knees to the feet, are also black.

A 'brown' pony is like a very dark bay. A 'dark brown' is nearly black but has a brown muzzle. A 'black' (as coal) pony is very rare.

Chestnut ponies come in three main shades: bright chestnut, light chestnut and liver chestnut. Their manes and tails can be chestnut-coloured, flaxen, auburn, or even dark grey.

bright chestnut

light chestnut

liver chestnut

A dun pony can be golden, silver, yellow, or 'mouse' (also known as 'dark'). He nearly always has black legs. He also has a dark stripe along his spine from his mane to his tail. It is known as an 'eel stripe'.

golden dun

silver dun

yellow dun

mouse dun

A palomino (which is a *colour* not a breed) generally has a light golden coat and a cream mane and tail.

Grey coats will lighten with age, so a pony who looks as white as snow is still described as 'grey'.
Grey ponies are light grey (which really looks like white), iron grey, dapple grey (like a rocking horse) or 'flea-bitten' (grey, with small brown flecks).

light grey   iron grey   dapple grey   flea-bitten grey

A pony whose coat is a basic grey thickly mixed with another colour is called a 'roan'.
A 'blue' roan has blue-grey hairs mixed with white or black, and sometimes also with pink.
A 'strawberry' roan is grey or white flecked with a pinky-red colour which looks like mashed strawberries.

    blue roan   strawberry roan

When you are describing piebalds and skewbalds, which are known as 'coloured' ponies, you can say 'white' instead of 'grey'. A piebald's coat is white with black patches. A skewbald's coat is white with either chestnut or brown patches . An 'odd-coloured' pony is white with patches in which two shades of brown merge into each other.

Last in this fashion parade are the rarer 'spotted' ponies. 'Blanket' spots are dark blobs on a white rump. 'Frost' spots look like a sprinkling of icing sugar on a dark coat. 'Leopard' spots are large, dark dots on a light coat. 'Snowflake' spots are white blobs on a dark coat.

In this book you have learned how to tell a healthy pony from one who isn't feeling well, just by looking at his coat. Later on in the Compass Pony Guide series you will learn how to care for his coat as well as his mane and tail, and how to make him look smart for a show.

A gleaming coat is the sign of a pony who is healthy because he is being fed the right food, which you can read all about in Book 7.

7. FILLING UP THE TANK

News Flash!

Flash!

Reporting the News

Sharon Hill

Contents

I. From News to The News

What is news?

News is coming at us all the time – on the radio, in the newspapers, and on TV. A news story can be about people, events, sport, or almost anything. It can be about something that happened today, last week, or last century. But to be news, it must have something *new* to say – new information, a new opinion, or a new way of looking at things.

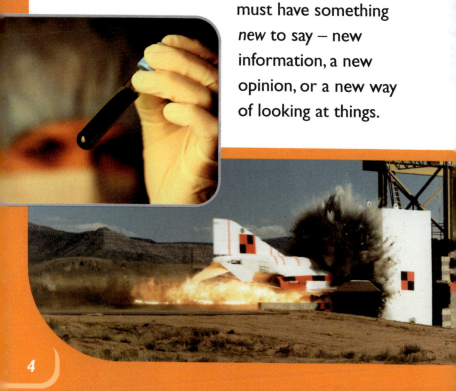

Where does news come from?

News reporters find news in many different ways. They may talk to people who have information about something that has just happened. They may get calls from people with news. Often reporters first hear about a news event or situation through a **press release**.

Creating a news story

Once a reporter gets a news **lead**, they discuss it with their **editor**. If the editor thinks that it will make a good news story, the reporter collects all the facts and they decide on an "angle".

The facts

When they are creating a news story, reporters use this checklist to make sure that they have included *all* the facts about an event or situation:

- *What* happened?
- *Who* was involved?
- *When* did it happen?
- *Why* did it happen?
- *How* did it happen?

The angle

The angle of a news story is the point of view or focus of the story. An angle helps to keep the story short and interesting. For example, for a news story about a football game, the angle could be that the winning team hasn't lost a game all season. Without that angle, the story might just be a boring description of the game.

News is only new for a short time. Reporters are always working quickly so that their story will be the first one about a news event or situation. This is called "breaking news" or a "news flash".

The birth of a news story

Here's a press release that was sent to the **news media** about an oil spill in New Zealand. The following chapters look at how reporters, from radio, a newspaper, and television, each used it to create news stories.

Press release

A ship has spilled oil into the sea near the Poor Knights Islands, a popular fishing area and marine reserve. Rare birds and fish living there may be in danger from the oil. The ship that spilled the oil has not yet been found, but authorities are investigating.

2. On the Radio

Many news stories are reported first on the radio. That's because a radio report of an event can go to air almost immediately. Television news stories have to be filmed, and newspaper stories have to be printed, so there is always a delay.

News flash

The first news report on the Poor Knights Islands oil spill was from radio reporter Lois Williams. Lois, who lives near the islands, got a phone call late at night from a **contact**.

After finding out as much as she could about the spill, Lois quickly wrote a voice script. She then phoned in her script to the radio station (even though it was the middle of the night). The news presenter read it on the next news bulletin.

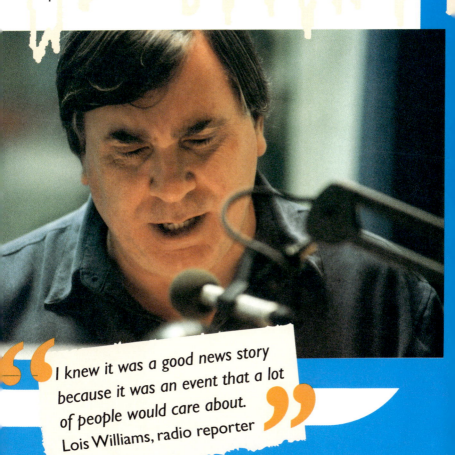

" I knew it was a good news story because it was an event that a lot of people would care about. "
Lois Williams, radio reporter

Features of a radio news story

Radio news stories are short – often taking less than thirty seconds. A radio voice script needs to explain the news event as simply as possible because listeners will get only one chance to hear and understand it.

- *Lead:* the first sentence of a radio story, telling listeners what the item is about and introducing the rest of the story

- *Voice script:* the story written and recorded by the reporter

- *Sound bites:* recordings of people talking about the news event

- *Lockout:* the final words, giving the reporter's name

- *Wildtrack:* background sounds, recorded out **in the field**, to make the story more realistic.

A reporter combines the voice script with the sound bites and wildtrack, and the story is ready to go **on air**.

SLUG   AUTHOR TIME (2000) MOD AUD DUR CUME   B/TIME
DU OIL SPILL WILLIAMS/Dec 03 1:45/03 1:55   0.47
INFO:
H/L: CONCERN OVER OIL SPILL IN NORTHLAND WATERS.
                                    SUB: WILLIAMS

Environmental agencies in Northland are on full *lead*
alert, after an oil spill near the Poor Knights
Islands.

The Northland Regional Council says the spill is
several miles across; it appears to be bilge
discharge from a ship, and it's heading for the
marine reserve, east of Whangarei. *Voice script*

Tony Phipps, of the council says the slick is
a mixture of light oil and large, tarry lumps
- and these could damge the fragile marine ecology
if they reach the Poor Knights.

He says the two ships were seen heading north,
off the east coast last night, and the Maritime
Safety Authority is investigating to see if either
is responsible for the oil spill.

Meanwhile Regional Council and Conservation staff
are preparing for the worst: they're taking out
boats at first light to assess the damage to the
marine reserve, and rescue any oiled birds.

In Whangarei, Lois Williams *lockout*

13

Follow-up stories

Over the next ten days, Lois filed several more radio stories about the oil spill. For these follow-up stories she had more time so was able to record her scripts herself in an **audio suite**.

The angles that Lois used in her radio stories were:

- the effect of the oil on the environment and the clean-up effort

> *I rang Wade Doak, who's been diving at the Poor Knights for forty years. He was very upset at the mess the oil had left in one of his favourite spots, the Rikoriko Cave. I used a recording of him talking about the cave in one of my stories.*

- the possibility of boats being banned from the islands
- the identity and prosecution of the boat owner who dumped the oil.

3. In the Paper

Most newspaper stories are longer than radio or TV news stories and so can give more information. Gathering all the facts for a written news story can be a big job, especially if the story is going to press the same day.

First story: big news

Newspaper reporter Tony Gee first heard about the oil spill near the Poor Knights Islands when a contact phoned him.

> I knew that this was a good story because the Poor Knights Islands are one of the top places in the world for diving. I knew that an oil spill there would interest lots of people who care about the environment.

The editor of his newspaper decided that the most attention-grabbing angle would be to focus on the ship that had dumped the oil.

Tony spent a long time getting facts and quotes from people over the phone. He arranged for a photographer to take pictures of the oil spill. Once he had all the information he needed, he wrote a story and faxed it to his newspaper's **subeditor**. The subeditor decided to make it the lead story. The **lead story** needs to be big, so the subeditor combined Tony's story with one written by another reporter, Jason Collie.

To catch readers' attention, the subeditor put a photo of an oil-covered bird in the top-left corner – the part of the page where most people look first. The paper's graphic designer produced a map of the area, and the subeditor wrote a headline. The story wasn't published until the second day of the oil spill. The reason for the delay was because the newspaper comes out in the morning and reporters did not have enough time to do a story for the first day.

picture

headline

byline

intro

caption

High seas hunt for oil-dumpir

By TONY GEE ar

An internation for an oil slick Islands.
Patches of oil kill seabirds and world-famous n
Thick patche bays and inlets on Thursday.
It is believe from a passing stage was 7km wide.
The island unique and er plants and were rated servationist J as among th spots in the
Marine Wade Doak the interna Rikoriko C bomb had
There all over the said from Aorangi.
Wind a yesterday continue line befo
The M Council e northeas compan
Depa birds co of the
Mr I quate with c oil. An Poor F

CASUALTY: Alan Fleming and other Conservation Department staff are w___g to save wildlife from the oil slick which washed into the Poor Knights Islands. They expect birds that congregate around the islands to continue to be caught in oil patches.

18

Features of a newspaper story

- *Headline:* draws attention to the story and captures reader's interest

- *Byline:* the name of the writer

- *Intro:* a summary of the story, so that the reader can decide whether they want to find out more

- *Pictures:* photographs, maps, or sketches to break up the written text and give visual information about the news event

- *Caption:* words explaining the picture

- *Quotes:* what people have said, word-for-word – backing up the story with people's direct experience of the news event.

Second story: a new angle

On the fourth day of the oil spill, the wind started to blow the oil away from the Poor Knights Islands. Tony and his editor decided that this was a good angle for another story that would be very different from the first one. Tony wrote less **copy** this time and decided that a photograph wasn't needed. Because it was smaller and had a less exciting angle, the subeditor placed this story on page 4.

Poo

Oil dam

By TONY GEE

WHANGAREI — W
Poor Knights Isla
reserve from the
quences of Thursda
"The impact cou
lot worse if calm
tions had come ea
Northland Regio
monitoring manag
yesterday.
"It's a tragedy
any oil in a marin
were saved to so
wind."
Regional cou
ment of Conse

Knights saved by wind

could have been worse

decide today whether to continue cleanup work or let clumps of oil disperse naturally through wind and tides.

An inspection of the caves and bays is to be made this morning, after the major environmental scare, when large areas of floating bilge oil from a still-unidentified ship threatened marine and bird life on the isl... ...m from Tutukaka off... ...and east coast.

A ma... ...ation was launched ... ...to clean u... spilled so... washed as... ber of se...

on the western side of the islands.

Suspicions are focused on two ships, which will be asked to provide samples of bilge oil for comparison.

Mr Phipps said five or six more dead oil-covered birds, probably shearwaters, had been picked up from the sea during the weekend.

A smaller number of dead and injured oiled birds, including penguins and the Bullers shearwater species which nests only on the Poor Knights, were found on Fri... ...day. More dead birds are expected

the most effective cleanup method was to do it manually.

"We couldn't use skimmers or booms on the open sea in wind and we couldn't use a lot of equipment in the caves and bays on the islands."

He estimates cleanup costs so far at between $30,000 and $50,000.

Northland-based diver, marine conservationist and author Wade Doak said yesterday that the best outcome to the incident would be to become better prepared in future.

"I'm not knocking the guys working out there cleaning up. They've been doing their best but it's a matter of finding the best methodology to handle this sort of

Friday, what was happening is open to criticism. If nets and buckets are effective [in scooping up spilled oil] then it would be more effective to have more than just one or two boats doing it.

"We need someone in the country who knows all about oil spills and who has no axe to grind to come up with some strategies."

A voluntary code has existed since 1994 for oil tankers allowing captains to choose whether to go out to sea round the Poor Knights or cut between the islands and the mainland — a distance of 9 nautical miles.

Many skippers take the easier, direct route inside the Poor Knights.

...would push for these guy... to ... w extra miles around the K... said Mr Doak.

The good thing about newspaper stories is that you can reread them. You usually get only one chance to see or hear the news with TV and radio news stories.

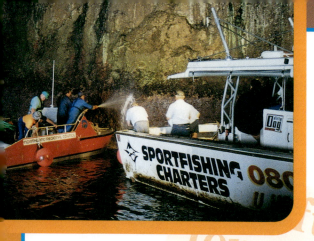

Third story: end of story

The next day, people began cleaning the oil out of coastal caves. Tony and his editor decided that this was a good angle to take for one more story. The story was about the same length as the second one but included a photograph.

The oil spill was less interesting news now, so the subeditor placed this story on page 6.

Several small articles on the spill were written later by other reporters on the paper. News about the oil spill lasted in the newspaper for about three weeks. This is longer than it lasted on both radio and TV.

4. On the Screen

Television is a very powerful way of reporting news because people can actually see things happening. TV news editors prefer stories with some action that will look interesting on the screen and those that can be filmed easily. TV stories need to be easy to follow, but they can still give a lot of information because they use pictures, sound, and text.

POORER KNIGHTS

On the spot

TV reporter Kim Hurring was on her way to work when she heard about the oil spill on the radio. So when she was asked to report on it, she already knew a bit about it. She had most of the day to do a story for the TV news programme that night.

Kim phoned a few people who had information about the spill, then she and a camera operator went to the islands by helicopter and boat. They filmed shots of the area and the oil in the water.

Filming for TV

The camera operator tries to get many different "general" shots of the whole scene as well as close-up shots of people involved in the news event. Filming interviews requires close-ups and wide shots of the person talking and some shots of the reporter. TV news stories are less than four minutes long, so only a small amount of the footage that the camera operator shoots will be used.

After talking to lots of people, Kim filmed interviews with just three of them: a person who was trying to save birds from the oil, a tourism boat operator, and a boat owner who was helping to clean up the oil. Finally, she did a piece-to-camera, which she'd written just before it was filmed. Piece-to-camera scripts are often written on the spot so that they are right up to date.

Mike Thorsen
DOC

Back at the TV studio, Kim edited the story with the video editor in the editing suite. They put together the best shots of the island, the piece-to-camera, and the interview footage so that the whole story looked good and was easy to understand. Kim wrote and recorded a voice-over to fill in the gaps and explain the pictures.

Graphics were added, and the story was ready just in time for the evening news programme. After all that effort, it was just two minutes ten seconds long, but it was important enough to be the second news item.

Features of a TV news story

- *Lead-in:* the story introduced by the news presenter before it is screened
- *Graphics:* any writing, charts, or maps

- *Voice-over:* the voice speaking while the film is shown – written and recorded by the reporter, usually after the pictures have been put together

- *Caption:* the words along the bottom of the screen, usually naming the person being interviewed
- *Interview:* film footage of the reporter talking to someone about the news event

- *Piece-to-camera:* the reporter talking directly to the camera about the news event, usually on the spot
- *Sign off:* the reporter giving their name and TV station.

Follow-up story

There was only one more TV news report on this event, the next day, which focused on the hunt for the ship that had spilled the oil. So the story had a short life on TV, compared with radio and newspapers. Kim says that you can never tell how long a story will last on TV. Some start small and grow bigger, and others start with a bang and then die away like this one did.

The Life of the Story

Media: Radio
First report: Friday morning
Life: 10 days
Reasons for life: Human interest
story (about people)
Local reporter on the spot
Radio stories can be short bursts
of new information

Media: Newspaper
First report: Saturday morning
Life: 3 weeks
Reasons for life: Local reporter
Human interest story (about people)
Newspaper stories are longer
and can give more information

Poor Knights
Oil damage could have been

Media: TV
First report: Friday evening
Life: 2 days
Reasons for life: Reporter didn't
live in the area
Action didn't last long

Glossary

(These words are printed in bold type
the first time they appear in the book.)

audio suite: the room where the audio producer edits sound

contact: a person who phones a reporter with breaking news

copy: the text of a news story

editor: the person who decides what goes into the newspaper, the TV news, or the radio news and chooses stories and angles with the reporters

footage: an amount of film or videotape

in the field: outside the studio

lead: a piece of information that might lead to a story

lead story: the most important news story, at the top of the front page of a newspaper or the first story on the TV or radio news

news media: organisations that publish news

on air: being broadcast on radio or television

press release: a statement given to the news media

subeditor: the person who edits a reporter's story, writes the headline, and decides where it will appear

Index